Voices of Henry Street
Portrait of a Community

Photographs by **Harvey Wang**

Preface by **Richard Abrons**

Introduction by **Brendan Gill**

Historical Essay by **Judith Ann Trolander**

Published by Henry Street Settlement, 1993
265 Henry Street, New York, NY 10002
(212) 766-9200

Preface
Richard Abrons

This is a book about the Henry Street Settlement. Not about its history or its programs or its facilities. It is a book about some of the people whom the Settlement has impacted and who have in turn left their mark on the Settlement. It is a book of piercing photographs by the immensely talented Harvey Wang accompanied by carefully chosen selections from interviews and, in some cases, from several hours of oral history recounted by each person.

It is a book of old and young, of Black, Latino, White and Asian, of Board and Staff, of club members, music students, homeless, youth at play.

Why create such a brief book to commemorate Henry Street's hundred years of service? I only wish we had such a book forty-five years ago, when I was a counselor at Camp Henry, or in 1896 when Lillian Wald came to minister to my grandmother's struggling family on Attorney Street. For there have been plenty of histories, plenty of documentation. This book captures the spirit of Henry Street. You read it with your heart.

In its essence this book is a poem, a hymn, a painting. It is a work of art. And Art has always been central to the Henry Street experience. Sixty years ago, Lillian Wald wrote, *"the development of the arts at the House has been, I think, our most stirring and rewarding adventure..."*

Open this book and experience some of that adventure.

Richard Abrons is President of the Henry Street Settlement Board of Directors.

Introduction
Brendan Gill

We Americans have always been notorious for our optimism. The older cultures of Europe and Asia have mocked our conviction that by the exercise of a few simple principles—hard work, bodily discipline, kindness to others—we could insure a steady improvement in the social conditions under which we live. This optimistic conviction, however innocently embraced and pursued, has led in some instances to success of a high order—success that no one has reason to mock. One such instance is the Henry Street Settlement, which for a hundred years now has devoted itself continuously to bettering the lives of others.

Ironically, the success achieved by the Henry Street Settlement serves to make clear that the optimism felt by nineteenth-century Americans was—shall we say?—in most cases over-optimistic. For the social problems that the Henry Street Settlement confronts and strives to resolve today are every bit as difficult as those that Lillian Wald confronted and strove to resolve in 1893. They have not been caused to wither away; on the contrary, certain contemporary problems of ours may be more difficult than any that existed in the past, as being greater in number and more complex in nature.

To speak of numbers, the proportion of foreign-born in the population of New York City is almost exactly what it was a century ago. In terms of the proportion of those of our native-born who are impoverished or unemployed, the situation is, if anything, worse than it was a century ago. Moreover, the number of entry-level jobs capable of being filled by functionally illiterate people diminishes from year to year. In the nineteenth century, immigrants who could neither read nor write English could get jobs digging ditches and performing other manual labor on their way up the so-called ladder of opportunity. Today no ditches are dug by hand, and the skills required to manipulate an industrial robot tend to make us suspect that robotic skills may soon exceed our own, rendering all of us, workers and thinkers and writers alike, superfluous.

The electronic age and its requirements are not sympathetic to the poor, the uneducated, the disease-ridden, the drug-addicted. We perceive with reluctance that the Statue of Liberty does not, in fact, raise her lamp beside a golden screen. Never in its long history of service has the Henry Street Settlement been so indispensable—a part of the social fabric of New York City—indeed, of the whole country. The newly completed restoration of its handsome buildings (ancient by our New York City standards) is a symbol in bricks and mortar of the diligence with which the Settlement goes about weaving and reweaving that ever-in-jeopardy social fabric. In Harvey Wang's superb photographs, we come face to face with some of the actual weavers of the fabric — men and women who in so many cases began their relationship with the Settlement in childhood and have strengthened their bonds with it day by day from one decade to the next.

These weavers are, in effect, our surrogates when we provide financial support for the Settlement. Turn the pages of this book—this family album that is at once sentimental and as hard as nails. We may not have been lucky enough to be photographed by Harvey Wang, but if we are among those who have helped the Settlement achieve a long and fruitful past (and intend to help it achieve a similarly long and fruitful future), then we are already members of the family.

Brendan Gill is the architecture critic for New Yorker Magazine *and is the author of many essays and books about New York City.*

A Historical Glance

Judith Ann Trolander

"A sick woman in a squalid rear tenement, so wretched and so pitiful...determined me, within half an hour, to live on the East Side," wrote Lillian Wald in describing the impulse that prompted her to start Henry Street Settlement in 1893.

Wald was then a young nursing school graduate taking courses at the Women's Medical College, when she became interested in the home nursing needs of immigrants on New York's Lower East Side. She originated the idea of visiting nurses actually living in the neighborhood of their patients. Joined by her friend, Mary Brewster, and financed by banker Jacob Schiff and others, the two women moved into the top floor of a rented tenement on Jefferson Street in the fall of 1893 and began what originally was called "Nurses Settlement." At that time, the concept of the visiting nurse was just beginning to emerge, and settlement houses were just starting to get established. Wald was unique in blending both ideas.

By the time Nurses Settlement opened its doors, more than half a dozen settlement houses were operating in the United States. The purpose of the settlement houses was to meet the needs of their poor neighborhoods in two ways. The first was by providing immediate services on a daily basis, usually of an educational/recreational nature. The second was to bring about fundamental social reforms. The settlement philosophy originally held that if middle class residents and staff actually lived in the neighborhood that they were serving, their relationship would be more equal with those they sought to help. They would also gain added insights into the causes of poverty, and have an added right in seeking to improve neighborhood conditions as members of the community. People, who were attracted to the settlement idea by its novelty and exciting prospects for social reform but who didn't want to change their middle class lifestyles, could volunteer, usually to teach a class or lead a club. By 1893, cities were separating themselves into neighborhoods by social class. The settlement

Lillian D. Wald

idea was to encourage contact among diverse groups. Most settlement neighborhoods, like the Lower East Side, were filled with immigrants attracted to America as the land of opportunity. Settlements gave these immigrants the chance to take English and citizenship classes, attend neighborhood concerts and dances, and meet with people who had succeeded in America. In fact, from the beginning, they provided a meeting ground for people from diverse ethnic, racial, religious, and social class backgrounds. Nurses Settlement was no exception. From the start, it contained a dynamic mix of individuals.

In 1895, banker Jacob Schiff bought Wald a three-story, Federal-style, row house at 265 Henry Street, which is still the administrative center of Henry Street's operations. Two additional buildings at 267 and 263 Henry Street were later obtained in 1908 and 1934 respectively. Schiff was a German-Jewish immigrant who achieved success as a financier and then became a leading philanthropist specializing in Jewish cultural institutions. When Henry Street incorporated with a formal board in 1903, Schiff was one of the most prominent members and his continued connection served as a reminder of the potential opportunity America held for the Settlement's immigrant neighbors. Schiff's son-in-law, Felix Warburg, served on the Henry Street board with him and his grandson, John Schiff, who became president of the board in 1937. Today, another Schiff descendant, Mrs. Frederick Warburg, is an honorary director and still another, Dr. Andrew Schiff, recently joined the board. Other board members with deep roots at Henry Street are Hyman Schroeder, a member of the American Heros Club, Henry Street's first youth group, and a lawyer named Samuel Schneeweiss, both of whom took part in activities while growing up in the neighborhood. All did more than give Henry Street money; their personal success was an inspiration to the Lower East Side neighborhood, and it was through the board that they continued their connection with the area.

The settlement house also offered its staff (in the early years most came from middle class backgrounds) a unique opportunity to explore their own potential. The most charismatic staff member of all was Lillian D. Wald, the daughter of a seller of optical goods who had a cultivated up-bringing. She was twenty-six when she founded Henry Street, remaining as head until her retirement in 1933. At home with all social classes, Wald had the ability to win financial support for innovative projects, carry them out, and convey an image of strength and commitment that was equalled only by Jane Addams of Hull House in Chicago. A gifted writer, Wald wrote two books The House on Henry Street (1915) and Windows on Henry Street (1934).

Wald attracted some distinguished residents to Henry Street. Foremost among these was Florence Kelley, head of the National Consumers League and a reformer dedicated to improving working conditions. Her father, William "Pig Iron" Kelley, so nicknamed because he strongly promoted the interests of the steel industry, served thirty years in Congress. Florence Kelley had studied abroad, become a socialist, and earned a law degree.

263-267 Henry Street

She was extremely outspoken in contrast to Wald's more gracious manner. Together the two made a formidable team as they led investigations, publicized the results, and lobbied to end child labor, bring parks and playgrounds to the Lower East Side, promote pacificism, and combat racism.

The results of their efforts made Henry Street one of the most influential settlements in Progressive Era reform. The visiting nurse service idea caught on and spread. The Henry Street nurses were available on a nonsectarian basis to low-income people, who were only charged what they could afford. The nurses saw the need for preventive health care through education and also instituted a program to seek out tuberculosis patients, providing them with disinfectants and other help. When Henry

Street proved the worthiness of this program, the New York City Department of Health took it over in 1905.

This demonstration project method of reform worked well. In 1895 to get children off the streets, Wald set up one of the first playgrounds in New York in the Settlement's three backyards on Henry Street. She was also a force in the creation of Corlears Hook and Seward Parks. In 1902 to convince the city to adopt school nurses, Henry Street paid the salaries of the first ones and demonstrated that these nurses reduced truancy related to illness. Other school services offered early at Henry Street were kindergartens, adult education, and special education for the retarded. Henry Street's vocational counseling service was one of the first when it began in 1920. It later became the Vocational Advisory Service, operating in connection with the New York State Employment Service. In 1906 when social services for African Americans were frequently ignored, Henry Street opened Stillman House -- later called Lincoln House -- on West 60th Street. By 1925, twenty-six people or one-fifth of Henry Street's staff were African American.

Although the Lower East Side is frequently thought of as a Jewish neighborhood because of the large influx of immigrants from 1880 to 1920, the area was, and still is, quite diverse. Reformer Jacob Riis, Lillian Wald's contemporary, photographed residents who were Italian, Greek, Chinese, and African American. At Henry Street, these people had access to social clubs, classes in carpentry and photography, a gym, neighborhood dances, festivals, and an unusually high quality performing arts program. Beginning as volunteers in 1904 by offering dance and drama lessons, Rita Wallach Morgenthau and Alice and Irene Lewisohn, members of two prominent New York families, launched the Neighborhood Playhouse, a nationally recognized little theater in 1915. Henry Street began its Music School in 1927. After World War II, Alwin Nikolais gave considerable artistic stature to the Henry Street Dance School. Then in 1975, the facilities of the theater on Grand Street were enhanced with the addition of the Abrons Arts Center. The Settlement's arts programs have always brought people from different backgrounds into direct contact with each other. In fact, the diversity of the neighborhood was the theme of the settlement's twentieth anniversary street pageant in 1913.

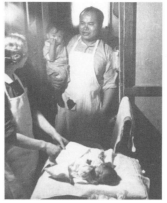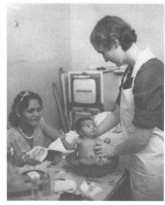

Founded as a visiting nurse service in 1893, Henry Street quickly expanded to become a comprehensive social service and arts agency.

Under Lillian Wald, both the settlement program and the visiting nurse service flourished. By that twentieth anniversary celebration, the Henry Street Visiting Nurse Service numbered ninety-two nurses. In additon to the public health nurse and the school nurse, Wald established a milk station in 1903 that made quality milk available to convalescents and babies. While well-baby clinics and similar activities were common in other settlements, none provided health care on the scale of Wald's Henry Street. When Wald retired in 1933, the Visiting Nurse Service had grown to 265; it numbered 300 nurses at the time of her death in 1940. Administratively, the Visiting Nurse Service had become increasingly independent of the settlement and in 1944 the two became two separate corporations, the Henry Street Settlement and the Visiting Nurse Service of New York.

In 1933 Helen Hall became the second executive director of Henry Street Settlement. The daughter of a small manufacturer, Hall had honed her administrative skills as head of University Settlement in Philadelphia where she also had the foresight to do a study of unemployment for the National Federation of Settlements called <u>Case Studies of Unemployment</u> (1931). Hall would also serve as president of the National Federation from 1934 to 1940. On moving into the headworker's apartment at Henry Street, the forty-one-year-old Hall eagerly greeted her new neighbors, urging them to make her feel at home at 265 Henry Street.

Helen Hall

Hall's arrival also marked a new era in social reform. Although Lillian Wald had helped to establish the Federal Children's Bureau, her political efforts had focused primarily on the local and state level. The New Deal, however, rapidly shifted the welfare burden to the federal government and Hall was part of that shift. She served with her soon-to-be husband, <u>Survey</u> editor Paul Kellogg, on the Advisory Council on Economic Security, making recommendations for the Social Security Act, the foundation of our welfare system today. She was unhappy about the exclusion of national health insurance, but continued to do studies and campaign for better health care. When Lyndon Johnson signed Medicare into law in 1965, Hall was among the dignitaries rewarded for their efforts with an invitation to the signing ceremony.

In the 1930s and '40s, Hall frequently provided testimony to various congressional committees on social welfare issues. At Henry Street, she put the settlement's practice of doing surveys to support social change on a more institutional basis when she began the Settlement's Community Studies Department. Significant research efforts included a study on unemployment in 1933, another on housing conditions that was useful to reformers who campaigned successfully for public housing legislation, and a study of 553 low-income families who faced health care problems in 1950 and 1951. While these studies were not always very sophisticated in a statistical sense, Hall's aim was to personalize reality with descriptions of individuals experiencing the problems she was asking the government to rectify. Despite the fact that she achieved a great deal during her tenure at Henry Street, Hall chose to title her autobiography, <u>Unfinished Business</u> (1971).

Perhaps the most significant resident of Henry Street during Hall's leadership was Lillie Peck. The daughter of an Austrian immigrant, Peck had become the executive secretary of the National Federation of Settlements, and did much to strengthen that organization at the time that Hall was its president. Through her work, Hall was able to draw on a national network of fellow settlement workers in her reform efforts.

The postwar years brought about a new relationship with government agencies and public funding of social service programs. Henry Street was able to establish a mental hygiene clinic and the new public housing projects needed agencies to provide services for their residents. Again, Henry Street was in the vanguard. In 1957 Hall picked up on a suggestion at a Henry Street board meeting to create a program to saturate the Lower East Side with social services to reduce juvenile delinquency. The result was Mobilization for Youth, the prototype for the country's War on Poverty. Although the original idea of settlement-coordinated social services

The arts have been an intregal part of Henry Street since the 1890's.

failed to survive the planning state, Henry Street was a participant and staunch supporter of Mobilization for Youth in its federally-funded action phase. That program's confrontation-style approach to community organization was troublesome to landlords and school officials, but it was successful in reaching many residents of the Lower East Side who avoided more conventional organizations like settlements. When Mobilization ran into charges of radicalism and corruption, Henry Street was there to defend it. The subsequent War on Poverty elaborated on Mobilization's theme of involving the poor directly in policy-making through community action. When Hall retired in 1967, she yielded the reins of leadership to Mobilization's director, Bertram Beck.

Bert Beck was the first executive director of Henry Street to hold a Master of Social Work degree. Prior to coming to Henry Street, his cocerns combined an interest in key reform issues with the promotion of professionalism in the social services. Under Beck, Henry Street aggressively sought public funding for innovative human services projects. Of great significance was the development of an early transitional housing facility, the Urban Family Center, which not only gave families previously housed in "welfare" hotels temporary apartments, but provided many services to help these families improve their living skills so that they could secure and maintain permanent housing. By 1977, Beck had expanded the program to include one of New York's first publicly funded battered women's shelters. He also initiated a housekeeping service to allow the disabled and elderly to remain

Today, Henry Street continues to provide arts programs for thousands of New York City residents.

in their own homes. One of Beck's most important achievements at Henry Street was the creation of the Abrons Arts for Living Center, which in 1975 brought all of the Settlement's arts programs under one roof for the first time. Beck also made efforts to help Henry Street's neighbors in other ways such as the creation of Martin Luther King park which adjoins the Settlement, and his purchase of a building behind 263 Henry Street for a local health clinic which had been operating above a pickle store. As Beck succeeded in gaining more government funds, only one-third of Henry Street's $4.5 million budget came from private sources.

Since Bert Beck, professional men have continued to lead Henry Street Settlement. Frank Seever, head of Chicago Commons, ran the Settlement from 1977 to 1980. Dr. Niathan Allen became the first African American to direct Henry Street from 1980 to 1983. Management consultant Michael Frey took over for over a year in 1983. The present director, Daniel, - Kronenfeld - Henry Street's first "in-house" appointment -- assumed the position in 1985.

Like Beck, Kronenfeld had a Master of Social Work degree and had also worked at Mobilization for Youth. In 1972, Beck hired Kronenfeld to direct Henry Street's innovative Urban Family Center. As executive director, Kronenfeld continued to build upon the model and strengths of UFC by developing education and training and employment programs. By 1992 the Settlement had constructed Helen's House, a small shelter named after Helen Hall located on Henry Street especially for families with young

A young artist shows his work.

children. It was also providing social services for a new shelter in East Harlem, and had established a training institute for managers and staff of shelters throughout New York City and state in order for others to benefit from the Settlement's experience. Under Kronenfeld, Henry Street's budget doubled and a much needed renovations and refurbishing of the Settlement's landmark buildings was undertaken. The agency's youth division continued to grow and touch more disadvantaged children and teens with new initiatives in training/employment programs, pregnancy prevention, HIV/AIDS education and conflict mediation. Henry Street's long time concern with children's welfare and education has continued with the growth of the arts-in-education program and close partnerships with local schools and Community School District #1. Kronenfeld responded to the AIDS crisis by implementing new programs to deal with the epidemic in virtually every division of the Settlement and a new housing facility for families with an AIDS member is being planned. Kronenfeld has also continued Henry Street's tradition of political involvement, hosting a campaign appearance at the Settlement for Governor Bill Clinton in July of

1992 and, in January of 1993, discussing youth employment and education issues with Clinton at the pre-inaugural luncheon. Most importantly, however the Settlement has carried on the traditon of responding to the needs of people on the local level.

Henry Street has changed a great deal since Lillian Wald's day, but much continuity remains. Danny Kronenfeld still lives at the settlement, a practice that has become extinct among other settlement heads. The Henry Street dining room is still a meeting place for people from many backgrounds. The community also remains very diverse, although the Eastern European Jewish immigrants of Wald's day are much diminished; the 1990 census revealed the neighborhood to be 32% Latino, 29% white, 27% Asian, 8% African American, and 4% other. The arts, music, dance, and drama programs are still strong. To them have been added more social service programs to deal with problems of family violence, aging, AIDS, literacy and homelessness.

Today, a translation of Henry Street's schedule of activities is available in Spanish and Chinese. As a Chinese/Puerto Rican woman who grew up at Henry Street to become a Civil Court attorney, Sue Ann Hoahng, recalled, *"The ethnic mixture of Henry Street was so diverse, yet we all got along. The Henry Street Settlement taught us to respect each other's culture and to learn from the differences."* One hundred years later, the spirit of Lillian Wald lives on at Henry Street.

Dr. Judith Ann Trolander, Professor of History at the University of Minnesota-Duluth, is the author of Settlement Houses and the Great Depression (1975) and Professionalism and Social Change: From the Settlement House Movement to Neighborhood Centers, 1886 to the Present (1987).

Voices of Henry Street

Portrait of a Community

.

Ecology Leader

Don't let the cool gaze fool you. Neriza Candelario is deeply involved in changing her neighborhood and her world. A lifelong resident of the Lower East Side, she is an alumnus of Henry Street Settlement's Cadet Corps, a youth leadership program, and a sociology major at the State University of New York at Purchase. In 1992, she was selected as an intern to help lead the Settlement's Greening Project, an environmental summer work and education program for 18 young people on the Lower East Side. Project members learned composting and gardening and organized a local recycling project. They took workshops in environmental issues, re-searched and visited the huge landfill at Staten Island, and expanded their horizons in a trip on the Hudson River Sloop Clearwater. Neriza's report on the project was enthusiastic: "The Greening Project definitely changed the young people who worked on it. When they first came, they said vague things like they wanted to make the world a better place. Now they have real environmental awareness. They tell their parents, `Don't buy this! It's polluting! Buy that!' They understand that to make changes in the envi-ronment, you have to do things differently and do them for a long time, until they become habit."

Neriza Candelario

Attorney

Samuel Schneeweiss, a prominent Manhattan attorney, grew up in a crowded railroad flat tenement on the Lower East Side where, Schneeweiss says, "we were lucky to have a private bathroom." He first attended Camp Henry in 1929, when he was 10 years old. After that came a time when, he recalls, "I was spending almost all my free time at the Settlement." He participated in clubs and studied acting, speech, puppetry, pottery, metal work, and photography. As a college student, he worked at the Settlement as a receptionist and switchboard operator, making $18 a week, "which was as much as many married men at the time." He also returned to Camp Henry for several years as a counselor and by 1940, was making $100 for the summer, a considerable sum.

In 1948, Helen Hall wrote of Schneeweiss in a letter, "of the hundreds of young men who pass through our doors, he is one of the highest caliber and among the most promising." Schneeweiss was an active member of the Cooperative and Savings Club which became the Henry Street Settlement Credit Union. He served as an officer and director of the Credit Union for many years. A member of the Settlement's board of directors from 1952 to 1979, Schneeweiss has been an honorary member since. He is one of very few who can still recite the chorus to the "Mother Henry Song" ("Mother Henry, we'll remember you when other memories fade...") written for Lillian Wald, founder of Henry Street Settlement. "We sang it when she visited us at camp on Sundays," he said. "And when she didn't."

Samuel Schneeweiss

Family In
Transitional Housing

On a bone-chilling February night, the apartment of Marisol Perez and her four children at Henry Street Settlement's Urban Family Center is warm, inviting, and smells deliciously of the family dinner. Giving up a chair to a guest, Perez explains, "I came here from Puerto Rico when my daughter, Thay-leng, turned out to have a life-threatening heart condition and needed an operation. At first we stayed with my brother on Clinton Street, but he became ill and couldn't keep us. I tried staying with other relatives and was all through the shelter system before I got in here. I wish I could stay here permanently. I feel protected and safe here, and I'm close to Bellevue Hospital where my daughter goes."

The Urban Family Center was founded in 1972 as one of the city's first transitional housing facilities for homeless families. Its comprehensive programs have helped more than 5,000 families move into permanent housing.

One thing Perez doesn't understand is why her apartment, with its neat-as-a-pin furnishings and framed art, surprises visitors. "It's bad enough to be poor and not have your own home," she says. "Why would anyone choose to be dirty too?"

Marisol Perez , Thay-leng , Jonathan .

Sport Story

"Am I a good player? Let me put it this way," says Roland Thomas. "People enjoy watching me. I can play down low in the guard, I can dribble, I can shoot." But while sports may be a metaphor for life, Thomas and the rest of his Operation Athlete teammates at Henry Street are learning that they need more than athletic gifts to reach the stars.

Orlando Mitjans, a former New York Giant who heads the Operation Athlete program, explains, "We're trying to keep these young men and women in school so that they can get into college. We get them tutoring, we coach them for their college aptitude exams, and we take them on trips so they can see what college life is about."

For those like Chauncey Joye, the combination of athletic and academic coaching is critical. Chauncey says, "Henry Street helped me get a summer job and get back into going to classes. We have a good team here, but the help I'm getting in school is just as important as playing."

Operation Athlete Team members. Kneeling in middle: Chaucey Joye. Kneeling far right: Roland Thomas.

Home Industry

The sewing machines and carpentry tools at Henry Street Settlement's Home Planning Workshop are getting on in years, but 400 local residents are still saving money and getting pleasure from using them. Ruth Taube, director of the workshop since 1965, explains, "Neighborhood residents come here to sew their own curtains, drapes, clothing, and slip covers, and also repair furniture electrical appliances and shoes." She adds, "The workshop's family atmosphere lends itself to friendly discussions about everything from simple soup to sex to politics."

The Home Planning Workshop has undergone an evolution since it was founded in 1940 to help tenants in the neighborhood's newly built public housing projects make their own furniture. At that time, tenants fashioned their beds, couches, chairs, and kitchen cabinets from the models and equipment supplied in the workshop. Today, Taube points out, "Lumber is so expensive that people can't afford to make their own. They look for sales on used furniture instead."

Pat Brown, a local resident, comes to the workshop about three days a week. "I like to sew and create things," she says. "I recently made a $200 coat for $40." Taube helps to support the program by running a thrift shop at the Settlement, which raises about $7,000 a year from donated items. "I give very much of myself to this program," Taube says, "but I also get so much from my friends here in return."

Left: Ruth Taube. Right: Pat Brown.

Property Manager

When his family moved from the Dominican Republic to the Lower East Side in 1963, nine year-old Rafael Jaquez thought the United States would be a place where "there was no dust and everything was shiny and made of glass and chrome." Instead he found a neighborhood steeped in poverty and drugs. He swept and mopped floors in the building in this photograph, where his father worked as a superintendent. At 15, while looking for a summer job, he met the director of Henry Street Settlement's youth division, the late Jim Robinson, who persuaded him to join the Cadet Corps, a youth leadership program.

At Henry Street, Jaquez signed up for a fencing class, thinking he would pick up a practical skill — putting up fences. The misunderstanding shaped his early life. He started an after-school fencing program at Seward Park High School and earned a first individual place in a citywide competition, while his team took second overall. In 1976, as a student at St. John's University, Jaquez earned a berth on the Olympic fencing team.

As a member of Henry Street's Youth Council, Jaquez became the first youth representative to vote on the Settlement's board. He established a Youth Enterprise Company that secured jobs so young people could finance a cultural/educational experience in Puerto Rico. He served as resident counselor in Henry Street's group home for boys and assisted in organizing the Settlement's Brother 2 Brother program, which encourages teen fathers and pregnant girls' boyfriends to face their responsibilities and relationships. Now a property manager, Jaquez also teaches at Columbia University and at the Harlem Children's Aid Society. He still quotes the Cadet Corps credo, "Enter to learn, go forward to serve," and his attitude towards youth is that he "believes in them."

Rafael Jaquez

A Settlement Family

Henry Street Settlement has been a long-time family affair for Debbie Cox, her mother Hazel, her sisters Theresa and Michele, and the six Cox grandchildren. Debbie is now a computer instructor in Henry Street's Youth Employment Service, which helps train and place low-income young people in jobs. Her son, Wayne Casimir, is in the day care program, which Debbie knows she can trust, having been a toddler there herself. "I remember it very well," she says, "especially the day we got filmed to be on `Sesame Street!'" As public school students, Debbie and her sisters enrolled in Henry Street girls' clubs where they learned cooking, family life and cheerleading. As a teenager, Debbie joined Henry Street Settlement's youth leadership program, the Cadet Corps, and at 17, she became a senior scout, a Pioneer. Her mother was in the Cadet Corps parents' group.

"I didn't want to join Pioneers at first because they seemed so serious," Debbie says. "But Jim Robinson, the head of the program, was like a father to me, and he talked me into it. I'm so glad he did because I really learned a lot there." In addition to her full-time job, Debbie works with the New York City Department of Health to organize performances and activities for an annual AIDS awareness day in a local park, to which her friend Fab Five Freddie, host of "MTV Raps," helps bring in star performers.

Standing left to right: Hazel Cox, Theresa Cox, Debbie Cox-Langley, Frank Langley, Michelle Cox. Sitting left to right: Wayne Casimir, Rodney Hopkins, Taisha Dunston, Michael Cox (sitting on lap), Shaun Cheeseboro, Cornell Cox (sitting on lap).

Leadership and Partnership

Youth empowerment is a buzzword today, but when Winslow Carlton, former president of the Henry Street board, took the leadership in founding Mobilization for Youth back in the red-baiting 1950s, some people got the program confused with communism and screamed to shut it down. Carlton recalled, "We wanted to overcome juvenile delinquency by encouraging indigenous leadership on the Lower East Side. I don't think we were as effective as we hoped. But the program did become the basis for President Johnson's War on Poverty programs and the progenitor of today's community legal services."

During the Depression, Margaret Carlton worked in partnership with her husband on President Franklin Roosevelt's Self-Help Cooperative Program. In the mid-1950s, she headed the Henry Street Settlement board's fund-raising efforts and in 1963, launched the planning and funding that eventually led to building the Settlement's Abrons Arts Center in the 1970s. That effort was kicked off with a 50th anniversary art exhibition commemorating the famous 1913 "Armory Show" of European art. For the past 15 years, the Carltons have lived in Woods Hole, Massachusetts.

Winslow and Margaret Carlton.

Theater Director

Essayist, short story writer, author, producer, and director, Woodie King, Jr. has enlivened Henry Street with his formidable talents since 1970, when he joined the Settlement as director of cultural arts. With the encouragement of then-executive director Bertram Beck, King founded the New Federal Theatre. "We wanted to create a theater for writers who had not had a voice, people of diverse cultures who could create plays that spoke to the diversity of the Lower East Side," King recalled.

During the theater's first season, King produced four plays in the basement of St. Augustine's Church on Henry Street. Later, the theater moved to the Henry Street Playhouse on Grand Street. When the Abrons Arts Center was completed next to the Playhouse, King and his company filled the new space with workshops in acting, directing, and playwriting. Over the past 22 years, the company has produced more than 150 plays.

King has produced many Broadway and off-Broadway plays, including *For Colored Girls Who Have Considered Suicide When The Rainbow Is Enuf* and *What The Winesellers Buy*. He directed and co-produced the film *The Long Night* in 1976, was nominated for a Joseph Jefferson Award in 1985, won an AUDELCO Award in 1986, and won the NAACP Image Award for his production of *Checkmates* in 1988. King has written a number of books, contributes essays to drama reviews and professional journals, and has had his stories collected in distinguished anthologies, including Langston Hughes's *Best Short Stories by Negro Writers*.

Woodie King Jr.

Flute Teacher

"I don't feel it's my job to train the next flute section of the New York Philharmonic," says Sam Baron, who has nonetheless taught some of the nation's leading flautists at Juilliard and the State University of New York at Stony Brook, where he is on the faculty. "If I train somebody who doesn't go into music, who teaches in their own neighborhood or plays for their own pleasure, there's still intrinsic value in it. Music itself is a value."

After a childhood spent listening to his uncle, a cantor, sing traditional Jewish melodies, and some years of violin study, Baron came to Henry Street Settlement's music school in 1942 to learn the flute. He remembers the star-studded orchestra that Robert Scholz had assembled at the time. "The violinists included Burl Sonovksy, Charles Libo, David Navian, and Stuart Cann," he says. "They were very competitive with each other. When there was an orchestra rehearsal and the conductor called a break, these guys would get up, run out into the hall, and challenge each other to play rapid things, like four-octave scales or the cadenza of the Tchaikovsky concerto."

A year after he completed his flute studies at Henry Street, Baron was accepted at Juilliard and invited to join its music school faculty. He stayed for 20 years.

Sam Baron

Celebrating Diversity

Have you ever laughed at an ethnic joke? Were you angrier when Rodney King was beaten than when Yankel Rosenbaum was shot? Are you self-conscious when you're the only person of your race or gender in a large group? The Cultural Harmony Theater group will make you laugh and gasp and cheer, at the same time that they invite you to explore your attitudes on these most personal and public of subjects.

The troupe's talented teens spent the summer of 1992 at Henry Street's Youth Program, composing a play, *I Like My Feet Because I Dance,* under the guidance of playwright Robbie McCauley. The play consists of a series of fast-paced, dramatic vignettes on such themes as inter-racial dating, black-on-black crime, and personal violence. Several key vignettes are open-ended and conclude by inviting the audience to finish the scene.

Now directed by Verna Hampton, the troupe performs in schools, community centers, and neighborhood theaters. When Nydia Velazquez, the newly elected U.S. Congresswoman from Manhattan, saw it, she was so moved she asked to have it presented at the Federal Courthouse, in honor of her induction.

Cristina Chang, 18, who has been with the troupe from the beginning, says that the play has helped her deal with her ambivalence about being of mixed racial origins. Chang says, "Racism hurts people a lot but they don't often talk about it. In this program, we have an opportunity to get those feelings out in the open."

Cultural Harmony Theater group: Verna Hampton, Muhith Ahmed, Nicole Clemens, Joel Rivera, Tanisha England, Shaheeda Yasmen-Abdush Shaheed, Christina Chang, Yuberkis Perez, Bernard Valentin, Elizabeth Caba, Vivian Olvera.

Actor

Nine years into his tenure at the Henry Street Settlement Playhouse, something was bothering director Joe Balfior. The year was 1962. "We had students from all over New York City — except for local minority children," he remembers. "The Playhouse seemed off limits to members of the community." With the encouragement of Settlement assistant director Ruth Tefferteller, Balfior rounded up the local youngsters and divided them into two age groups, each of which performed a musical — and another, and then another. And so, Pete's House Productions, named after the Youth Center building at 301 Henry Street, was born. Over the next five years, Pete's House Productions offered hundreds of city youth the opportunity to express themselves on stage.

Balfior recalls seeing Shelley Winters, Celeste Holmes and Yip Harburg at the shows. Richard Rodgers came often, too. "It was such a touching thing to see him," Balfior says. "He would pat each kid on the head at the end of the show when they walked past him in the aisle." One of the children's biggest fans was then-Governor Herbert Lehman, whose son was the namesake of Pete's House. "I remember the governor attending one of our productions in a wheelchair," Balfior says. "He was only supposed to stay for the first act because he was so ill, but during intermission he argued with his wife about it, and stayed to see the end. I thought that was a wonderful compliment to the kids."

Joe Balfior

Dance Pioneers

He calls himself an abstract expressionist, says his dances center on "motion, not emotion" and considers the scores he composes to be "sound rather than music." A pioneer of modern dance, Alwin Nikolais became the director of the Henry Street Playhouse in 1948. For the next two decades, the Nikolais Dance Company, with its star dancer, Murray Louis, revolutionized the medium, exploring abstract movement in a multimedia theater of light projections, puppetry, electronic music and inventive costumes. While dance aficionados thronged the playhouse for the troupe's avant garde offerings throughout the 1960s, city youth found its way to the stage through the children's dance program that Louis directed there. The generation of modern dancers who studied with Nikolais included Phyllis Lamhut, Louis Falco, and Twyla Tharp.

Today, "Nik" and Murray are co-choreographers of the renowned Nikolais and Louis Foundation for Dance. Even in his early sixties, Louis is still dancing effortlessly, choreographing new pieces for what he calls "a new range of movement." *New York Times* reviewer Jack Anderson might have been describing the duo's lifelong collaboration in a recent review, when he noted that their dances spring from "the simple pleasure human beings take in amazing one another."

Left: Alwin Nikolais. Right: Murray Louis.

Electrical Engineer

"A lot of kids today don't think they have a future. They don't think that there's anything left for them," says Anthony Noel, an electrical engineer with Con Edison and a Henry Street Settlement board member. Noel has been working with young people at the Settlement since 1981, the year he graduated from Columbia University.

A descendant of former slaves from Suffolk, Virginia, and Cariacou, a Caribbean island, Noel is the first professional in his family. He was introduced to Henry Sreet by a friend when he was 17 and later became involved in the Settlement's Operation Athlete program, which encourages sports-minded young men and women to stay in school so that they can get into college. A junior varsity basketball guard in college, Noel counseled young people in Operation Athlete as an assistant coach and trip chaperone. He helped evaluate them academically, tested them athletically, and guided them either to athletic scholarships or whatever alternatives made the most sense. "Every day was a challenge to get them to understand they could trust us; we put our trust in them," he said.

It was at Henry Street that Noel first encountered young people from many ethnic backgrounds — African-American, Puerto Rican, Dominican, and others — and realized the universal nature of their problems. "When you let a young person down today, he is very hurt," Noel says. "I can see it as a result of the changing society. The young people are watching us. If we don't offer them any direction or role models, they'll fall right out of line, and that would be a terrible thing."

Anthony Noel

Artists In Residence

In the early 1980s, when Marina Gutierrez, Juan Sanchez, and William Jung were struggling young artists in need of encouragement and studio space, they were invited to set up shop in Henry Street Settlement's Abrons Arts Center studio as artists-in-residence. Sanchez recalled, "Henry Street gave us an open space where each of us was able to create our own workshop. We shared information and had conversations and fed off each other's work." Jung agreed, "There was a lot of camaraderie, with each of us coming from different cultures and meeting at Henry Street, which is itself a cultural crossroads."

Willie Birch, a lower East Side artist who already had an exhibition history, joined the program because of his interest in creating and directing a large-scale performance piece that drew on his African American and Native American roots. During his residency, he met Gutierrez and Sanchez, and they eventually all moved to the same tenant-owned and -operated apartment building in Brooklyn.

Gutierrez says, "For me, the important part of the Henry Street residency was the comradeship of people who were serious about their work. If you don't have that kind of example, the possibility of living your life as an artist always remains elusive." Now with many exhibtions, awards and national honors to their credit, all four have also become teachers -- Guitierrrez directs a model program for high school students at Cooper Union, Sanchez is a professor at Hunter College, Birch has been at the Guggenheim Museum/Learning Through The Arts and Jung works with the New York City Public Schools -- and relay these messages to their own students.

Left to right: Juan Sanchez, Marina Gutierrez, Willie Birch, William Jung.

Cook

Nora O'Malley began working at Henry Street in 1933 — the year Helen Hall took over from Lillian Wald and O'Malley arrived in New York from Ireland — and stayed for 39 years, outlasting even Helen Hall. "The cooking was pretty plain when Miss Hall was there," she says in an Irish brogue that's as strong as black coffee. "You had salad or soup and a nice dinner — meat and vegetables, fried or mashed potatoes, and we made a good cheese souffle." On St. Patrick's day, green jello was served.

Working fifteen hours a day at least six days a week, Nora and co-workers Sally Loftus and Peggy Staunton made breakfast, lunch, and dinner for about 30 staff members. "We worked hard all right," she says. "We had to make the ice cream by twirling it in a little machine, and we ground the fresh coffee and cut the meat by hand." Retired since 1972, she's still an active chef in her Woodside, Queens home, where she often entertains. "Now I mostly do chicken and pot roast—easy things."

Nora O'Malley

Day Care Leader

Sandy Lo Kwok, assistant director of Henry Street's day care center, understands the culture shock new immigrants experience. A native of Hong Kong, Kwok clearly recalls her arrival in Superior, Wisconsin as a college student in the 1970s. "The town consisted of a J.C. Penney's, two movie theaters, one of which was playing *Love Story* for six months, and a lot of German and Irish people who'd never seen anyone Chinese before. They stared at me like I was from outer space." Kwok transferred as soon as she could to Long Island University. She applied for a job at Henry Street Settlement in 1977, at a time when the day care program was seeking to reach out to the growing Asian population of the Lower East Side.

Now the mother of five children with one home in Chinatown and another in Brighton Beach, Kwok has a special empathy with the small Asian children in her program. "Staff often ask me to help if they're puzzled by a child's behavior," she said. "I speak Cantonese and a little Mandarin and I know the culture the children come from, so I can usually figure out what's going on in a few minutes. For example, some of them come from traditional families where they're taught not to look authority figures in the eye. That can make them appear to have emotional problems in an American context." A sign of Kwok's effectiveness is the growing appeal of the day care center for the neighborhood's Asian families. "When I came, enrollment was 10 percent Asian. Now it's 65 percent."

Left to right: Isaria Bueno, Leilani Cloud, Sandy Lo Kwok, Amanda Perez, Jesenia Fuentes, Janiece Dejesus, Jiallun Yee.

Riding on a Blue Note

A pianist and saxophonist from an early age and a friend of Charlie "Bird" Parker, Thelonious Monk, and other be-bop pioneers, Vincent Smith had the talents and interests of a jazz musician but decided instead to be a painter. He remembers Charlie Parker telling him, "Vince, stick to your vision; don't let nobody turn you around." It was sage advice. As a young black man from a poor Brooklyn neighborhood, Smith had few role models in the visual arts. In the 1950s, he studied briefly at the Art Students League, the Brooklyn Museum, and the Skowhegan School and immersed himself in the New York avant garde art scene. Later he became involved in the protest movements of the 1960s and 1970s and traveled to Africa — experiences that figure prominently in his rich, uniquely African-American visual vocabulary. In 1990, Smith's eighth solo show inaugurated the Master Artist Series of solo exhibitions at Henry Street's Arts Center. Called "Riding on a Blue Note," it featured his works on musical themes and was accompanied by a jazz presentation in the Arts Center's theater. Smith said, "Music has always been such a strong passion of mine, and this show at Henry Street was pivotal in my career. I traveled with the show to museums and galleries around the country for two years." Smith recently donated a monoprint to the White House on the occasion of President Clinton's luncheon invitation to Daniel Kronenfeld, Henry Street Settlement Executive Director.

Vincent Smith

Recalling the '30s and '40s

"If I let my fingernails grow, I could reach across it," said George Stoney, a distinguished documentary filmmaker and New York University professor, about his room at Henry Street in the late 1930s. "I had a meager bed, a place to put my portable Underwood typewriter, a chair, a lamp. Out the window, I had a view of a Hasidic synagogue, where the men would sing and dance around the Torah all night. For a kid from the South, this was all brand new."

Stoney's room and board at 301 Henry Street were free, in exchange for his work on pamphlets about social work research that the Settlement was conducting. Helen Hall hired him — a coveted assignment in the depths of the Depression — on the basis of a "suitcase full of columns" written for his hometown North Carolina newspaper. Stoney recalls meals in the elegant dining room in Henry Street's main building with such guests as mayors Fiorello LaGuardia and William O'Dwyer and politicians from England's Labour Party. "It was always very formal," he said. "I was often asked to sit at the head table because I was the `token' Southern liberal."

While at the Settlement, Stoney struck up a friendship with Betty Puleston that has lasted through their lives.   Puleston directed an after-school pro-gram and a summer day camp for children whose families paid 10 cents a week to enroll them. She also ran the Works Progress Administration school at the Settlement that provided jobs for artists and offered work-shops to some 300 adults, one of whom was Jackson Pollack. Stoney says, "Back in the 1910s and 1920s, Henry Street was already advocating the kind of programs that ended up in the New Deal. When you worked at Henry Street, you were on the cutting edge of what we then called social engineer-ing."

George Stoney and Betty Puleston.

Homegrown Board Member

"I like to think of Henry Street as the doors of change," says Julio Colón, who calls himself a "homegrown" member of Henry Street's board of directors. A Puerto Rican-American, Colón moved with his family to Henry Street at age 10, after his mother witnessed a gang war murder in their Brooklyn neighborhood. He discovered the Settlement a year later, when he joined a pottery class.

Colón's first impression of the late Jim Robinson, Henry Street's director of youth development, was the turning point in his life. "Jim saw me as a lost soldier," Colón says, "and gave me a real life battle to fight." His experience at Camp Henry was another powerful shaping force. Before his first trip there, at age 11, Colón was "overwhelmed that there might not be a brighter, greener, freer side to life." Later, he entered a counselors' training program and was exposed to new ways of thinking: "Black, Indian, Puerto Rican heritage, psychology, community organization, and physical, mental, and sexual discipline."

Colón became part of Henry Street's youth goverment, the Youth Council, and at age 16 was selected as a delegate to UNICEF, which Helen Hall helped found. Through the program A Better Chance, Colón attended a challenging New Hampshire high school. He earned a bachelor's degree at New York University in 1979 and a graduate degree at the university's Real Estate Institute. Instrumental in the founding and ongoing development of many community organizations, Colón is currently vice president of the Residential Mortgage Insurance Corporation. He says, "Henry Street gave me the room and the tools to grow. It gave me the forum to improve my life. That's what I see as Henry Street's legacy."

Julio Colón

Music Lessons

 Ask music teacher Louise Berhend about her most remarkable former students, and she'll mention David Herman, a violin maker and dealer who is also a painter. "He came to me when he was 12 years old. That's old for starting the violin. He was going to Yeshiva, which meant that he was in school from nine to six, and he was practicing four hours a day, which would make you remember anybody. He was so dedicated.

" Herman, now 49, says, "At the time, I wanted to be a famous violinist and I was fortunate to have Louise Behrend as my first teacher. I didn't have a chance to develop any bad habits." Behrend, who started teaching at Henry Street Settlement's music school in the early 1940s, introduced the Suzuki method to her students there in 1965. That made Henry Street the first music school in the city to offer Suzuki, which can be used to teach violin even to very small children. Now a teacher at Julliard, Behrend is also the founder of The School for Strings, where Suzuki method teachers are trained.

She said, "As the School for Strings evolved, I had teachers who needed experience, so I established something very much like the Henry Street program called the Special Program. It's designed for low-income students, so fees are very modest. That way, my apprentice teachers get their teaching experience —it's part of their training — and I make sure that every child has an opportunity to study."

David Herman, Louise Behrend and her Guarnerius violin.

Ending Homelessness

Is helping others the best way to help oneself? The women in this picture can testify that the old saw works. All are former residents of Henry Street's Urban Family Center (UFC), a transitional housing complex for homeless families. Now settled in their own apartments throughout the city, they have remained involved with UFC as paid case aides in the Self-Help Project, assisting UFC families moving into permanent homes with information, advice, encouragement, and referrals to services.

Norma Gonzalez, staff coordinator for the project, offers an example of a Self-Help assignment. "We just had a call from a former UFC resident who's received an eviction notice from her landlord. She refused to give the landlord the key to her mailbox and complained to the city about not getting heat or hot water. Her Self-Help case aide is going out there to help her fight the eviction and get the services she's entitled to."

Gonzalez says, "This project has had a tremendous impact on the case aides. Everyone now in the program is taking college courses. One went on to become a social worker and several have gone to permanent jobs at other places."

Left to right: Brenda Coaxum, Sebiila Jacobs, Ardella Brown, Bessie Webb, Theather Campbell, Agnes Rivera, Julia Vargas.

Family Service

"Henry Street Settlement's location in a small pocket of the city, cut off from mass transportation, created its own small world," says Mary Jones. Although that world on the Lower East Side was a far cry from the rural Virginia in which Jones was raised, she immersed herself in the Settlement during her 30 years as a board member, and encouraged her children, Dale Burch and Anthony Winslow Jones, to explore the Settlement. Dale Burch is now vice president of the board and chairman of the steering committee for Henry Street's Annual Art Show. To Dale, "The most important thing Henry Street does is put families back together and back into society. To me, that is certainly rewarding." Tony Jones, now also a board member, is a documentary filmmaker. He was active in a Henry Street film club during the 1970s and is now involved in the Arts Center.

In Mary Jones's days at the Settlement, her favorite programs were the dance performances of Nikolais and Louis, which were "brilliant — no one ever wanted to leave" and Good Companions, a program for seniors. "You walked down the steps to Good Companions and opened a door and there were these old people who looked young," she reflects. "They had a terrific social life with big birthday parties and weddings, music and games, and if anyone was ill they visited them. I was there many times with [Mayor] Bob Wagner, and he thought it was the most inspiring thing he'd ever seen. I took people from the U.N. to Henry Street and it inspired them too, because it gave them ideas of what they could do when they went home."

Left to right: Anthony Winslow Jones, Mary Jones, Dale Burch.

Battered Women's Shelter Director

Juanita Colón's childhood unfolded in tenement apartments on Rivington Street, Broome Street, and in the Lillian Wald Housing Project. At the time, the Lower East Side was still primarily Jewish and her family was one of the few that spoke Spanish. Colón joined the Henry Street staff in 1969 without a high school diploma but with "a dream of becoming a bilingual social worker." Later, she became a founding staff member of the Urban Family Center (UFC), which provided New York City's first transitional housing and comprehensive services for homeless families.

While living, working, and raising her family at UFC, Colón completed her master's in social work. In 1980, she became director of the Battered Women's component of UFC, one of the first publicly funded housing programs for battered women in the city. "My education as a social worker took place at UFC," Colón said. "It offered a rich environment to experiment and learn which has always made working there exciting." Colón feels that the settlement offers a special facility for homeless families "because we treat every individual with a sense of respect and dignity. Part of UFC's philosphy is that there is strength in everyone and our job is to look for it and nurture it."

Juanita Colón

Old Timers

Jacob Patent, Nathan Cheshes, and Sam Eppy are three of five surviving members of the Wilson Club, one of more than 100 clubs for Lower East Side youth that were formed at the Settlement beginning in 1895. Founded in 1916 for 10- to 12-year-olds, Wilson Club members met weekly during the school year to play sports, socialize, and occasionally hold dances with girls' club members. During the summer, they went to the Settlement boys' camp, Camp Henry, while the girls went to Echo Hill Farm — experiences many recall as the highlight of their young lives.

"The Wilson Club had interesting leaders," says Cheshes. "One of the earliest was Mrs. Slade. She was very elegant—a real socialite. Another was A. A. Berle. In later years, he became involved with the Roosevelt administration and was the ambassador to Brazil. He used to bring us apples after every trip he took. The leaders gave us advice and helped mold us."

The other Wilson Club survivors are Bernard Marks and a Florida resident, Joe Landres. They have sustained lifelong friendships and, like many other club alumni, continue their affiliation with Henry Street through the Old Timers Association.

Left to right: Jacob Patent, Nathan Cheshes, Sam Eppy.

Love Story

Linda Slade has been blind from birth, a disability that entitled her to receive home help from New York City once her daughter, Kelshia was born. But Slade found that many homemaking assistants were more trouble than caring for her baby alone. She was ready to do without help when Francisca Rodriguez, a Henry Street housekeeper, showed up. Slade recalled, "Mrs. Rodriguez's job is classified as `housekeeper,' not a home health aide, so she's not supposed to be doing child care. But my baby fell in love with her right away, and she wanted to help." Rodriguez bathed Kelshia, taught her to eat with a spoon, and took her to her own apartment to play with her grandson, born two years before Kelshia. When Kelshia began to talk, she called her "Digas," a nickname that's stuck. Rodriguez says, "At first I wasn't sure about working with someone who was blind, because I never did it before. After 10 years , we've become family."

Left to right: Linda Slade, Francisca Rodriguez, Kelshia Swanson.

Pioneer

Luz Herrera, a senior at Seward Park High School, moved from Puerto Rico to the Lower East Side at age 12. She struggled with English and felt out of place in the bilingual class she had to attend to finish sixth grade. She also noticed that "a lot of kids were selling drugs, hanging out late, smoking, stuff like that. I just wanted to stay away from all that."

A cousin told her about the Henry Street Settlement Pioneers, a youth leadership program that is the senior division of the Henry Street Cadet Corps. "I am a shy person who keeps a lot of things in," Luz says. "In the Pioneer meetings, we had to go around and say our names in front of the whole group. I would get nervous, my heart would beat. Now in meetings, I can talk and express my feelings."

After Luz completed a summer of work in the Pioneer program, Nilsa Pietri, chief administrator of youth services, offered her an after-school office job at the Settlement's youth center. She now works five days a week for Orlando Mitjans on the youth center staff, giving some of her salary to her mother to help at home. Still attending Pioneer meetings twice a week, Herrera plans a career in computers or modeling.

Luz Herrera

Artistic Direction

When John Morning joined Henry Street's board of directors in 1968, he "had only the foggiest idea of arts in a community setting," as he put it. But as one of New York's most distinguished graphic designers, his involvement was sought by Bertram Beck, then executive director, who wanted to strengthen the Settlement's leadership in the arts. "Bert is an extraordinary, very compelling individual," Morning said, "and seeing the arts flourish in that type of context proved very meaningful to me."

Morning, former art director at McCann Erickson and a trustee of Pratt Institute, says: "The mission of community art goes back to the very beginning of Henry Street. Lillian Wald had a belief that the arts were valuable for all people, that no one should be deprived of music or drawing lessons just because they were economically disadvantaged. I admire the fact that Henry Street's programs are very high caliber. Students at Henry Street see the work of professionals. They might say, `Wow, that's great, I want to be able to do that.' Or `This is something I never even dreamed about.' That's part of the process of education in the arts, introducing people to the best work that's around."

John Morning

Five Photographers

Today they're important photographers with major magazine credits, but you have to picture them back in the 1950s, when they were skinny, tough Lower East Side teenagers in garrison belts and motorcycle jackets. Classical music and painting were for sissies but photography was hip, with its sleek apparatus and jargon, and at Henry Street they could do it practically for free. They never heard of role models, but they looked up to their teacher, Nellie. She knew her stuff and she encouraged them. With their De Jur 2-1/4 cameras, donated to Henry Street by a benefactor, they snapped big guys playing basketball, sunset at the Brooklyn Navy Yard, boats steaming up the Hudson. The images blossomed in Henry Street's darkroom and, prodded by Nellie, they entered the best of them in a show at the New York Coliseum. Time-Life staff members who judged the show ended up hiring John Iacono and Manny Millan, who have been at Sports Illustrated ever since. "At one point, four of us were on the staff of Time-Life," recalls Iaccone. Says Neil Leifer, "There were other photography programs in the neighborhood, but for some reason, this one worked. It was a tiny program, but it produced five successful photographers." No one is quite sure why, but they're inclined to give credit to Nellie.

Clockwise, from top: Neil Leifer, Vincent Nanfra, Manny Millan, Mike Palmeri, John Iacono.

Civil Court Attorney

Sue Ann Hoahng, a court attorney for the Civil Court of New York, writes: "Henry Street Settlement House was a very important part of my growing up experience and not just mine, but my entire family's, my brother and my four sisters. I was part of the play school program after school, the Pied Pipers Summer Day Camp Program, and the different arts and crafts programs. My family was able to get out of the city through the Echo Hill Farm day outings. If it were not for Henry Street, my family would probably never have gotten out of the city during the summer. My father, who didn't speak much English, helped organize and participated in the first ethnic fair that the Settlement House sponsored. He cooked all the Chinese food and helped with the making of the Dragon. I am Chinese and Puerto Rican. My family was one of the first interracial families on the block. The ethnic mixture at Henry Street was so diverse, yet we all got along. The Henry Street Settlement taught us to respect each other's culture and to learn from the differences." Hoahng now lives in Brooklyn but has left Henry Street a tangible sign of her years there: a ceramic giraffe she made for the children's wall in front of the Settlement's building at 301 Henry Street.

Sue Ann Hoahng

In Harmony

They hail from different cities, generations, and musical backgrounds and had never met before this picture was taken, yet the former and current directors of the Henry Street Settlement music school, Robert Egan and Paul West, are in perfect harmony on the philosophy of the school. "It's one of inclusion and service," says West, a classical violinist and jazz bassist. "We're trying to develop people, not artists."

Egan, now a professor at Duquesne University School of Music in Pittsburgh, made changes at Henry Street in the late 1950s and early 1960s to accomodate the shifting ethnic make-up of the community. "We brought in performances designed to appeal to the growing black and Hispanic population, and eventually they responded," he said. When West came in 1967, he launched workshops in jazz and Latin music, Chinese and Japanese music recitals, an annual jazz concert series that featured such performers as Dizzy Gillespie, and a program of fully staged operatic productions.

West, who has played and recorded with Billie Holiday and Ray Charles, supervises instruction in 16 different instruments and voice, but feels that teaching music is only a small part of his job. "I'm a social worker, father, mother, psychiatrist, doctor, nurse, and friend," he says. "If students leave here as fully responsible, happy people, and attribute some of that to what they experienced here, I'm happy."

Left: Robert Egan. Right: Paul West.

Board Member

With five children and ten grandchildren, Isabel Potter has achieved a kind of domino effect during her forty years as a board member at Henry Street Settlement. "I've taken my children and grandchildren to Henry Street many times," she says. "My daughter-in-law, Ann Patterson, is an artist and a set designer who teaches in the schools, and my niece, Carol Irving, is a sculptor who was an artist-in-residence at the Settlement. Years ago, one of my daughters wrote a paper on the Settlement House, and she became a sociologist. Another daughter who is a lawyer is running a homeless shelter. Henry Street has inspired all my girls — they're all involved in the humanities, and each has a very strong social conscience."

Potter recalls her friend Helen Hall, executive director at Henry Street Settlement from the 1930s through the 1960s, as a legend in her lifetime. "She was a very strong personality. If she told you to go and do something, I'm telling you, you did it. She told me that when she was in the Red Cross in Australia during World War I and nothing was getting done, she'd go to General MacArthur and say, `I want a tent put there,' and believe me, it'd be up in seven seconds."

Isabel Potter

Youth Patrol

Mike Nixon's long career of commitment to youth and community began in 1957, when he became a police officer in the 7th Precinct, which serves the Lower East Side. As a community relations officer, he hosted weekly dialogues at Henry Street Settlement, co-moderated by Henry Street staff and aimed at helping the community, especially its young residents, feel that the precinct was an open place that belonged to the neighborhood. Nixon and other police officers took young people on weekend fishing trips to Camp Henry, helped establish the Youth Council at Henry Street, and acquired an unused firehouse on Broome Street as a site for youth activities.

Henry Street recommended Nixon for an award from the One Hundred Association in 1972. The award brought him to the attention of the mayor, who appointed him Ombudsman for Juvenile Justice. Since trading in his policeman's cap, Nixon has worked as director of Spofford Juvenile Detention Center, assistant commissioner of recreation for New York City, president of the NAACP Mid-Manhattan branch, and director of a Children's Aid Society neighborhood center. Currently deputy director of Riverbank State Park, Nixon has touched countless youth in New York City as their advocate, protector, and friend. He says, "I still think about Henry Street as the place that started me on the road."

Mike Nixon

Board Chair

Audrey Rosenman, chairman of the board of directors, first visited Henry Street as an eight-year-old during World War II. Her mother, Fannie Askin, was a longtime board member of the Settlement and brought her daughter to help show local residents how to use ration cards. Audrey worked as a camp counselor and was a member of the Friends of Henry Street before joining the board.

In the 1970s, as a student at the Columbia University School of Social Work, Rosenman was given a choice between writing a thesis and developing a project. Knowing that the Settlement was interested in starting a group home for adolescent boys, she decided to work with Henry Street staff to make it happen. The residence opened in 1972 on the fourth floor of Henry Street's Youth Center and accommodated about 15 teenaged boys at a time during its ten-year existence. "The boys could go to school on site at Henry Street and take advantage of all the arts and athletic opportunities that the Settlement offered," explained Rosenman, who served as the group home's president.

Rosenman is now a psychotherapist in private practice and a counselor at the Chapin School. Yet her work as Henry Street's chairman is hardly an avocation. "For the next ten days," she mentioned during a February 1993 interview, "only one day in my schedule is not involved with Henry Street."

Audrey Rosenman

Fix-it Men

High heels, loafers, boots, and oxfords are the province of Rigoberto Martinez, who runs the shoe repair service at Henry Street's Home Planning Workshop. The workshop dates back to 1940, when Helen Hall, then executive director of Henry Street Settlement, provided a space, tools, and materials for tenants in public housing to make their own kitchen cabinets and furniture. Today, the workshop still serves public housing tenants, but is devoted principally to sewing, woodworking, and repairs. Martinez dons his shoemaker's apron just three nights a week, but his low-cost service is so popular that customers are limited to only two pairs of shoes at a time. The equipment, donated by the Henry Street Old Timers Club, is "hard to get parts for, but still works beautiful," according to George Rosado, who likes to help Martinez in his free time. Rosado adds, "I could build my own house with what I've learned in this workshop."

Left: Rigoberto Martinez. Right: George Rosado.

Former and Current Directors

Bertram Beck, executive director of Henry Street Settlement from 1967 to 1977, dates his admiration for Daniel Kronenfeld, the current director, to the 1950s, when Beck was consultant for the TV series, "East Side/West Side," which starred George C. Scott as a social worker. Beck recalled, "I thought of Danny as the prototype for Scott's character. He had a successful but highly unconventional approach, more focused on product than process and, like Scott, he dressed more casually than your typical social worker."

The two men's tenures at Henry Street coincided in the early 1970s, when the New York City Human Resources Administration, plagued by scandals over the way it was housing families on welfare, turned to Beck for help. The outcome was Henry Street's Urban Family Center (UFC), an innovative program to provide decent transitional housing and 24-hour-a-day social services in a New York City-owned building. Sensing that the project needed a leader of uncommon skill and dedication, Beck named Kronenfeld, then a faculty member at Columbia University School of Social Work, as project director. Kronenfeld moved into UFC with his young family and stayed for 13 years — long enough to see UFC become a widely imitated model for housing homeless families and to be tapped as Henry Street's executive director in 1985.

Beck, now associate dean of the Fordham University School of Social Work, is proud of the successes he achieved at Henry Street and particularly so of building the Abrons Arts Center in the early 1970's in partnership with his wife Deborah. But he is awed at what Kronenfeld has wrought. He says, "When I see Henry Street alive with so many people and programs, and the amazing warmth with which everyone greets Danny, I think that Henry Street has found its ideal leader."

Left: Daniel Kronenfeld. Right: Bertram Beck.

Settlement Staff and Family

Parents often help young people get their first jobs, but Wanda Egipciaco's story is a twist on the familiar. She got her job as administrative assistant for the visual arts and arts-in-education program at Henry Street Settlement as a result of the long involvement of her two sons, Anthony and Javier, with the Settlement.

Egipciaco said, "As a single parent on the Lower East Side, I sent my sons to kindergarten at Henry Street, to the afterschool program, and to summer camp. When I had a car accident four years ago that made it hard for me to travel to work, I asked a staff member in the after-school program if he knew of any positions here. He referred me to the Arts Center and I've been there since."

Meanwhile, through Henry Street's Youth Program, the Egipciaco boys are able to see more of the world. Javier, 15, a visual arts student at Seward Park High School, has visited Aspen, Colorado twice through his participation at Henry Street — once for a summer environmental education program and once for a week of skiing. Anthony, 16, worked two summers ago as unpaid volunteer in the Settlement's arts day camp. The next summer, through the Youth Program, he got to spend six weeks in Hawaii. "There were seven of us, five girls and two boys," he recalled. "We helped set up a day camp program and we got to travel all over Oahu. There were beautiful beaches, great sunsets."

Left to right: Anthony, Wanda, and Javier Egipciaco.

Listening to the Children of AIDS

Lela Charney's warm, matter-of-fact manner is one of the assets she brings to her position as senior clinical supervisor and coordinator of AIDS services at Henry Street's Community Consultation Center (CCC). Another is her 18 years of experience working with troubled youth and adults at this pioneering mental health service, founded nearly 50 years ago by Helen Hall. Charney says, "The Center has grown enormously in the time I've been here. We've started a boutique business, The Unlimited, that gives clients real work experience, launched a dynamic and innovative mental health day treatment program, and responded to many crises in the community —AIDS among them."

Charney remembers well the telephone call she received in the late 1980s from a guidance counselor at a local elementary school. "She told me that nine children in the school had recently had deaths in their family. The children were running wild and obviously upset, and she wanted to know if I could help." When Charney and a colleague began doing group work with the children, they discovered that all the deaths were related to AIDS. Since then, group therapy for bereaved children has become an ongoing CCC service, a part of the agency's comprehensive AIDS initiative on the Lower East Side. "The children talk, read, draw pictures, celebrate holidays, and write letters to their deceased parents and to other children whose parents have AIDS," Charney says. "I think it's been quite an effective program."

Lela Charney

Two Brothers

In 1896, three years after Lillian Wald came to settle on the Lower East Side, she and Mary Brewster paid a call on a destitute widow with five children, one of whom was to become the mother of Herbert and Richard Abrons. Wald and Brewster tended a sick baby and gave the Abrons's grandmother sewing work that helped her get on her feet financially. It was the beginning of a relationship between Henry Street and the Abrons family that is now in its 97th year.

Richard Abrons is currently the president of Henry Street's board; Herbert is a former president and chairman. Their uncle, Hyman Schroeder, was known as "Miss Wald's prime minister." Wald herself called him simply "my son." Their father, Louis, namesake of the Abrons Arts Center, met their mother at a Henry Street dance. Herbert Lehman, a leader of a Henry Street boys' club and later Governor of New York and United States Senator, loaned him money to attend the University of Michigan.

In the 1930s, Herb Abrons led a boys' club at Henry Street. Both he and Richard worked as counselors at Camp Henry. Herb Abrons remembers holiday celebrations at the Settlement and coming home from Yale to dinner with Lillian Wald and her "wondrous ceremony of tossing the salad." Wald's picture graced their family den. "She was the quintessential mother — she exuded love," says Herbert Abrons. "When she spoke to you, it was as if you were the only person in the world."

Left: Richard S. Abrons. Right: Herbert L. Abrons.

Young Architects

These six fifth-graders are from a group of three classes at P.S. 110 on Delancey Street whose ideas have been transforming the dark drab walls of their entry/gym and lunchroom and a bleak square of concrete behind the school, into a bright and welcoming environment and an exciting playground. The students' teacher, Janet Sygar, launched the project in fall 1992 in collaboration with Henry Street arts-in-education instructor Joanne Yoshida. Through recommendations by the Settlement, the Sterling Foundation, an organization of professional volunteers, translated the students' ideas into professional architectural plans and then in an all-out community effort in May 1993, actually constructed the playground.

Janet Sygar says, "I've been working with Henry Street's arts-in-education program for several years, and it's always been a very successful collaboration. In addition to our two elaborate indoor murals, our architecture and design projects have included three illustrated Children's Walking Tour Guides of the Lower East Side. Students research their school and neighborhood and decide what they can do to beautify and improve it. Each year our graduating class gives the school a gift to leave it a better place." Says Joel Valentin, age 11, "When our playground is built, we're going to be so stunned we're not going to be able to do anything for a while. We're just going to stand around and say how beautiful it is."

Left to right: Joel Valentin, Janet Sygar, Jocelyne Serrano, Natalie Siregar, Michele Flores, Anganette Bracero, Benton Lee, Joanne Yoshida.

Education Worker

Grace Vargas, a classroom teacher turned staff developer in Community School District 1 on the Lower East Side, says: "I grew up in the 1970s in the Lillian Wald Housing Project on the Lower East Side, in a broken family of five on welfare. We were constantly faced with the temptation of drugs and alcohol, and the schools I attended on the Lower East Side did not address my social or emotional needs. Henry Street Settlement showed me that the only way out of my low economic status was by education, values and work ethics. I was part of the Pioneer youth program, which focuses on adolescent development and taught me how to work collaboratively.

"Working in the school district today, I'm trying to do what Henry Street did all along: to involve the community and the home in education, instead of seeing schools as a separate entity within the community. Henry Street Settlement shaped my philosophy as a woman, educator, mother and wife. It gave me the spiritual, social and emotional guidance to be where I am right now. When I go back there, it's like going home."

Grace Vargas

Two Cadets

Kim Lashley, 12, has friends who won't join the Henry Street Cadet Corps because they dislike wearing uniforms, but for her, the program has opened doors. "At first I didn't know anyone," Kim said. "Now I have friends from a lot of different schools. We play volleyball and double dutch. At the end of the year we do a program where we dance to hip-hop music. That's what I'm best at — dancing. Last summer, when Henry Street took us to Aspen, we slept in teepees, rappelled down a mountain, hiked, and learned ropes."

Jose Serrano, 11, remembers his fear that Cadets "would be like the army" but he's come to enjoy the rituals of uniforms and marching drills. He also likes the basketball, story-telling sessions, and trips. Last winter, his troop — B-company Boys — went skiing in Aspen. "It was fun!" he said. "I never skiied before. When I try things for the first time, I get over my fear."

José Serrano and Kim Lashley .

Education and the Arts

The further I get from the 10 years I spent at Henry Street, the more I realize how unique an experience it was," says Steve Tennen, who left Henry Street in the 1980s to become director of the Jamaica Arts Center. Tennen now heads ArtsConnection, the largest organization providing arts-in-education programs in the New York City schools. He recalls, "In the 1970s, when I came to the Settlement, the arts were disappearing from the public schools. With the opening of the Abrons Arts Center in 1975, we had something remarkable to bring the schools — a whole building devoted to dance, drama, music, and visual arts, that was there to stay."

Under the leadership of Mark Tilley, then Henry Street's arts director, Tennen supervised dance and drama programs for children, created a Family Theater that brought first-rate professional children's theater to the community, and helped found Henry Street's arts-in-education program, which continues to provide high-caliber art experiences to thousands of children in the public schools.

"The range of talent that came through Henry Street was vast," Tennen recalls. "We produced David Henry Hwang's `The Dance and the Railroad' which was John Lone's first directing effort. Denzel Washington played Malcolm X in `When the Chickens Came Home to Roost.' Phylicia Rashad did Zora Neale Hurston as a one woman show. The diversity was extraordinary, and so was the quality of the programs. Henry Street was all of a piece and it changed my life and informs the work I do today."

Steve Tennen

Having A Ball

Goldie Mendelson joined Good Companions, the senior citizens' program at Henry Street Settlement, just a year ago, in 1992, but her family feeling about the Settlement goes back for decades. Mendelson remembers: "I grew up on the Lower East Side in the Depression. As a little girl, I went to Henry Street's camp, Echo Hill Farm. Then in the 1940s, as the mother of a two-year-old, I joined a young mothers' club, The Women. We met every Tuesday night at Henry Street. We socialized, had guest lecturers, went to Broadway shows for 50 cents, square danced, raised money for charity. Every summer, we went to Echo Hill Farm with our children. We stayed five women to a room and had a ball! A group of us still meets at the Arts Center on Tuesday nights." Mendelson, an office worker most of her life, recently had to retire when the law firm she worked for closed its doors. She says, "Good Companions is saving my sanity. Everyone here is so active and up-to-the-minute. I come here every day God lets me."

Goldie Mendelson

Friends of Henry Street

A one-year subscription to Field and Stream. A $1,000 leather Batman jacket. A five day stay at Canyon Ranch spa. These are a few of the 250 goodies, contributed by donors from Kip Forbes to Christian Dior, that were sold at the Friends of Henry Street's annual fundraiser last Christmas. The sold-out affair at the Metropolitan Club featured dancing, a buffet dinner, gambling, and live music by the rap band Posse Deep and pop singer Brenda K. Starr. By party's end, thousands of dollars in net profits were added to the Settlement's coffers, which didn't surprise anyone at the spectacular bash dreamed up by this hard-working, under-40 fundraising committee.

The origins of Friends of Henry Street go back to Helen Hall's time, but this committee is especially up-to-date. "We have people who never turn us down when we ask for something," says Harry Slatkin, one of six co-chairs of the group, which has dedicated itself to continuing Henry Street's tradition of service.

Left to right: Lisa Jackson, Harry Slatkin, Alan Glatt, Barbara Page-Glatt.

Nuturing Talent

When Carmen Vega was a young child living with her family in the La Guardia Houses, her parents signed her up for dance, art, and cooking classes at Henry Street Settlement across the street. That's how she learned at an early age that she had a talent for visual art. Vega recalls, "At 14, I was given a job as an assistant in the Henry Street arts program, and by the time I was 16, I was making $5 an hour there. That was enough to pay for my own art supplies for my classes at the High School for Art and Design." Vega was also active in the Aspira Club, a Puerto Rican youth association founded at the Settlement.

After graduating from New York University with a degree in art and education, Vega returned to Henry Street as a full-time art instructor. She left in 1977 to become curator of the satellite galleries at the Bronx Museum of the Arts and then assisted the director of the museum, Luis Cancel, who had also taught at Henry Street and is now commissioner of the New York City Department of Cultural Affairs. She is now director of the East Harlem Tutorial Program, a comprehensive learning center that provides one-on-one tutoring and educational support to 350 primary school youngsters a year. "I always had leadership ability, but Henry Street developed it," Vega said. "Whenever I hear the name of Henry Street Settlement, I feel pride and joy."

Carmen Vega

Role Model and Learning

Nyrii Williamson, a junior at Washington Irving High School, devotes several afternoons each week to tutoring the children of families who live in transitional housing at Henry Street Settlement's shelter, the Urban Family Center. "I like to work with them and help them understand what they're doing in school," Nyrii says, taking a break from an arithmetic game she is playing with Anthony Reid, age 8. In another part of the room, a new six year old UFC arrival, is getting help with his spelling homework, and two tutors are taking turns reading a story to a group of girls. The children don't care much for interruptions, but Anthony does look up from his task just long enough to say, "I like doing my homework here 'cause when we finish, we get to play."

Donald Bennett, the UFC staff member who supervises the program in partnership with a Board-of-Education-licensed teacher, says, "We started the tutoring program to address some of the problems these children were having as a result of being homeless. After months or years in the shelter system, they need more than after-school caretaking. We're trying to give them the special attention and academic support they need to improve their work and self esteem and make a difference in their lives"

Left to right: Anthony Reid, Nyrii Williamson, Jennifer LaCarriere

Harvey Wang

Harvey Wang is a widely published photographer best known for *Harvey Wang's New York* (W.W. Norton & Co. 1990) a book of portraits of older New Yorkers whose occupations and way of life are being threatened by change. The highly acclaimed photographs were exhibited at the Museum of the City of New York in 1992, and in the words of the curator of the show, "was one of the most powerfully emotional and refreshing accessible exhibitions in the museum's history." Photographs from *Harvey Wang's New York* will be displayed at the National Museum of American History at the Smithsonian Institute in Washington D.C. in 1995. Mr. Wang has had exhibitions at the New York City Transit Museum, The South Street Seaport, and the New York Public Library. His other books are *Rock Wives* (William Morrow, 1986) and *Where Have You Gone Vince DiMaggio?* (Bantam Books, 1983). He is currently working on two new book projects. Mr. Wang's work has appeared in many newspapers and magazines and he has recently been filming documentaries for National Geographic's "Explorer" television series. Harvey Wang lives in Brooklyn with his wife Sonja and their daughters, Sakira and Sophia.

Acknowledgements

Many people have helped to make this project possible. Susan Fleminger, Director of the Visual Arts Program and Christopher Stevens, Associate Director of Development, organized and oversaw the development of both the exhibition and this catalog. As coordinator of Henry Street's Centennial, Kathleen Gupta, Director of Development, has been involved with the project from its inception. Jane Alpert was the chief writer of the profiles of the photographic subjects.

Henry Street Settlement would also like to thank the following individuals for interviewing and/or writing drafts of profiles of the people featured in the exhibition: John Berman, Louise Bobrow, Aimee Kaplan, Ingrid Melhus, Margot Mifflin, Renee Newman, Laurie Norris, John Petito, Greg Raynor, Candace Sorensen, Christopher Stevens, Harvey Wang, and Arlene Winer. Joan Dickson helped to recruit and coordinate the volunteers for the project and Arlene Winer gave two workshops on oral history techniques for the volunteers. Carol Sun designed and produced this exhibiton catalog which was printed by William Charles Printing. George Hirose and Charles Suddarth Kelly provided some of the contemporary photographs in the history essay and Emily Wolff helped research the photographs for that section and Steve Zeitlin of City Lore who recommended Harvey Wang. Finally, the Settlement would like to thank all of the participants in this project for taking time out of their busy schedules to be interviewed and photographed.

Generous funding for the exhibition and catalog has been provided by the J.M. Kaplan Fund, the Lucius N. Littauer Foundation, and the Henry Street Settlement Board of Directors.